Astronauts Take Flight

By Robert Gott

CELEBRATION PRESS

Pearson Learning Group

Andrew S. W. Thomas

★★★★★★★★★★★★★★★★★★★★★★★★★★★★★★★★★★★★★★★

born 1951

"If I could
go to the Moon,
I would do so
in an instant!"

★★★★★★★★★★★★★★★★★★★★★★★★★★★★★★★★★★★★★★★

Andy Thomas is from Australia. When Andy was a child, the first satellite was launched from Earth into space. The satellite was called *Sputnik 1*. One night Andy looked up at the sky. He saw *Sputnik 1* pass overhead. That is when he became interested in space and rocketry. Rocketry is the science of making and launching rockets.

Andy grew up to become a research scientist. He studied space and flight for many years. He became well known for his work.

Andy was chosen for training by the National Aeronautics and Space Administration (NASA) in 1992. NASA runs the U.S. space program and trains its astronauts. Andy became an astronaut after he completed the training.

He took his first spaceflight in 1996. Andy was the first Australian to travel in space. He then trained in Russia for a stay on space station *Mir*. Andy also learned to speak Russian so he could talk with the crew.

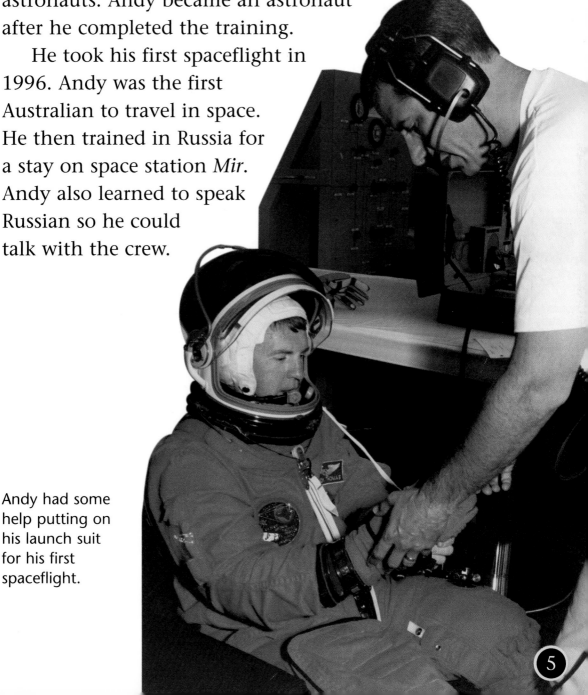

Andy had some help putting on his launch suit for his first spaceflight.

Andy lived and worked with other crew members on *Mir* for four months. Each astronaut had jobs to do. Andy did experiments on how space travel affects the human body.

There was not much room on *Mir*, but Andy said it was comfortable. It had a living area, exercise gear, small sleeping areas, and a toilet stall. Andy liked the fact that he didn't need a mattress to sleep. Feeling weightless was much softer!

On *Mir*, Andy ran on a treadmill to keep fit.

★★

⭐ Eating in Space

Imagine eating in a weightless environment where everything floats. Let go of a cereal spoon and it floats away. This would be a problem if tiny food crumbs floated off. They could get stuck in an astronaut's eyes or interfere with equipment. To help astronauts, food is carefully prepared. Salt and pepper are made into liquids.

Andy traveled to the International Space Station (ISS) in 2001. There, he became the first Australian to walk in space. He and another astronaut made the ISS ready for a new crew. They added parts to the outside of the ISS. They made a platform to hold a robotic arm from Canada.

Andy received many awards and honors when he returned from space. He also became deputy chief of the Astronaut Office at NASA. He now hires and trains astronauts. Andy is helping these young men and women reach their goal of becoming astronauts.

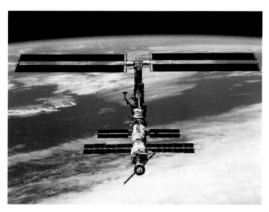

International Space Station

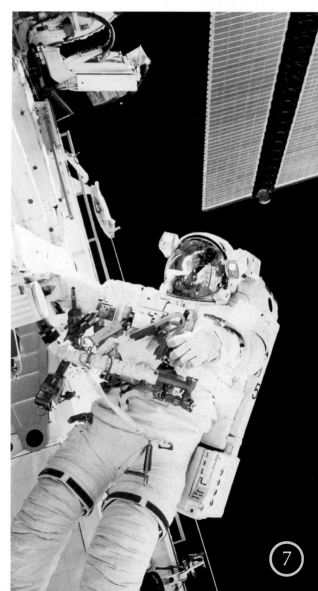

This is Andy on a spacewalk during his mission to the International Space Station.

Michael P. Anderson

born 1959, died 2003

"I take the risk because I think what we are doing is really important."

Michael Anderson was the son of a U.S. Air Force serviceman. He grew up near airfields where airplanes were always taking off and landing. When Michael was nine, he saw on television the first astronauts to walk on the Moon. He decided that one day he would be an astronaut.

Michael was African American, unlike his astronaut heroes, who were white. His parents encouraged him to work toward his goal. Michael never doubted that his dream would come true.

Michael took the first step toward his goal in college. He studied astronomy to learn about the universe. He knew that he would need an excellent understanding of science to become an astronaut. Michael graduated from the University of Washington in 1981. He became a pilot in the U.S. Air Force. He then taught other pilots how to fly.

NASA chose Michael to be an astronaut in 1994. He was on his way! His first space trip was on space shuttle *Endeavour* in 1998.

Michael stood with other crew members of the *Endeavour* flight in 1998.

The *Endeavour* shuttle crew had an important mission. The crew had to take astronaut Andy Thomas to space station *Mir*. They also had to deliver supplies to the space station.

In 2003, Michael was chosen for the crew of space shuttle *Columbia*. It was a science and research mission. Michael was in charge of the science experiments. He and the crew did more than eighty experiments.

⭐ Supplies to *Mir*

Michael Anderson was on space shuttle *Endeavour* for its first docking mission with *Mir*. *Endeavour*'s crew delivered more than 9,000 pounds of supplies and equipment to *Mir*. *Endeavour* is shown below *Mir* in this photograph.

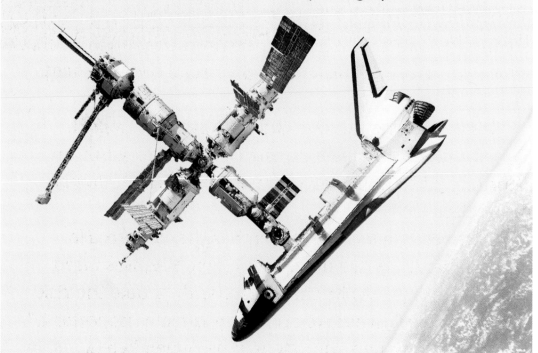

Michael set up several experiments on space shuttle *Columbia* in 2003.

Tragically, the mission did not end as expected. The shuttle broke apart during its return to Earth on February 1, 2003. All seven members of the *Columbia* crew died.

Michael Anderson is remembered as a hero. He worked hard. He did not give up when he was faced with challenges. As Michael once said, "I take the risk because I think what we are doing is really important." Michael's work and courage will be remembered.

Helen Sharman

born 1963

> "Science opens up new opportunities every day."

Helen Sharman did not set out to be an astronaut. She never thought that she would become the first British astronaut to go into space. Helen loved science. She studied chemistry at Sheffield University.

Her first job was with a technology company. It made equipment for ships, aircraft, and hospitals. Helen loved her job because she could use what she knew about science. Her next job was in a chocolate factory. She found ways to make chocolate quickly and cheaply.

One day, Helen heard an advertisement on the radio. It said, "Astronaut wanted, no experience needed." The ad was for Project Juno. Great Britain and the Soviet Union were gathering a crew for a space mission. They were looking for a person to be the first Briton in space. Helen wanted the job. She had to take many tests. They wanted someone who was calm and who worked well with others. The person also had to be strong and healthy. Helen had all of these qualities.

⭐ Helen's Passport and Clothes

Helen took a space passport on her mission. She would have needed it if she had landed in a different country than expected on return to Earth.

Helen's flight suit _____

Helen's space passport

FAI

МИР

№ 087

While on *Mir,* Helen performed experiments.

Helen was chosen from among 13,000 people to be the first astronaut from Great Britain. She was sent to the Soviet Union for training in 1989. There, she learned the Russian language. She also learned how to do scientific research in space. In 1991, she and two Soviet astronauts, called cosmonauts, were launched into space.

Helen spent six days on *Mir.* Space station *Mir* orbited the Earth sixteen times every day. While in space, Helen studied how weightlessness affects people and plants. She had to get used to the feeling of gravity again when she returned to Earth.

Helen wrote a book about her adventure called *Seize the Moment*. She said her life was nothing like she thought it would be. "Science opens up new opportunities every day," she said. Helen has been a writer, a speaker, and a radio broadcaster since her flight. One of her main goals has been to share the excitement of science with children and adults.

Helen had to regain her sense of balance after landing.

Marc Garneau

born 1949

"Going into space alters your perception. . . . You realize how important it is to take care of our planet."

Marc Garneau became Canada's first person in space. Marc did not plan to become an astronaut. He had a good job in the Canadian Navy. Then the United States invited Canada to send an astronaut on space shuttle *Challenger*. More than 4,000 people wanted to be that astronaut. Marc was one of six people chosen for training in the new Canadian program.

Marc used a camera for his work during one of his space shuttle missions.

⭐ Space Robots

Robots are nonhuman machines. They are used to explore space and to build and fix space stations. They perform tasks that might be too dangerous for astronauts. They can also do jobs that take many hours without becoming tired. The robotic camera Sprint, takes photos in space.

Marc spent eight days in space on his flight in 1984. He did experiments in medicine. He also studied how robots work in space. Marc also worked hard to help make the Canadian astronaut program a success when he returned to Earth.

Sprint

Marc wanted to fly in space again. In 1992, Marc was chosen by NASA to enter a special training program. He learned how to use many of the systems on a space shuttle.

Marc made his second flight in 1996. He spent ten days on space shuttle *Endeavour*. His third flight was also on the *Endeavour*. This time he helped build the International Space Station (ISS).

A 40-foot-wide drag chute on space shuttle *Endeavour* helped to slow it down on its return to Earth.

Marc no longer travels into space. He became president of the Canadian Space Agency (CSA) in 2001. It is a very important job. He helps decide what projects the CSA will do and how they will do them. One of Marc's goals is for Canada to become an important part of future missions to Mars.

In 2003, Marc spoke about Canada's plans for more space exploration.

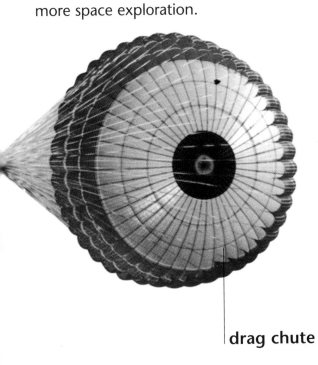

drag chute

France

India

Romania

Mongolia

Ellen Ochoa

born 1958

"Only you put limitations on yourself about what you can achieve. Don't be afraid to reach for the stars!"

"Don't be afraid to reach for the stars," said Dr. Ellen Ochoa. She did just that when she became the first Mexican American woman to fly in space. Ellen always loved math. She was an excellent student at her university. There she helped invent equipment that scientists use to look at images from space.

Ellen was chosen by NASA to train as an astronaut in 1990. Her math and science skills helped her as she studied and trained hard. Ellen became an astronaut in 1991. Then she began preparing for her first flight. She went on to make four spaceflights. Two of the flights were to the International Space Station (ISS).

Ellen played flute for the crew on space shuttle *Discovery*.

★★★★★★★★★★★★★★★★★★★★★★★

⭐ **Space Equipment**
Astronauts have to learn how to use all kinds of equipment both inside and outside the spacecraft. Ellen worked the controls for the robotic arm Canadarm on several space missions.

Ellen looked through a window of the International Space Station at parts of space shuttle *Atlantis* and the Earth beyond.

Space shuttle *Discovery* was the first shuttle to dock with the ISS. Ellen and the other astronauts prepared the ISS for the first crew to live there. Ellen has used a robotic arm called Canadarm on each of her flights. She used it to do work outside of the shuttle. On her first mission, Ellen captured a satellite that had been studying the Sun.

Between trips into space, Ellen works at the Johnson Space Center in Houston, Texas. She communicates with shuttles in space and helps guide astronauts. Her goal is to improve the ISS. She believes it is necessary for future space exploration. Ellen also enjoys talking to students about her career.

Ellen and another astronaut floated in one of the experiment rooms in the International Space Station.

Ellen talked about her 2002 flight experience on space shuttle *Atlantis* just after landing.

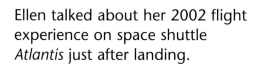

Index